Author's Note

From a young age, I was interested in animals, space, my surroundings—all the natural sciences. When I was a teenager, I became the president of a nationwide junior astronomy club with a thousand members. After college, I became a classroom teacher for nearly twenty-five years while also writing articles and books for children on science and nature even before I became a full-time writer. My experience as a teacher gives me the ability to understand how to reach my young readers and get them interested in the world around us.

I've written more than 300 books, and I've thought a lot about different ways to encourage interest in the natural world, as well as how to show the joys of nonfiction. When I write, I use comparisons to help explain unfamiliar ideas, complex concepts, and impossibly large numbers. I try to engage your senses and imagination to set the scene and to make science fun. For example, in *Penguins*, I emphasize the playful nature of these creatures on the very first page by mentioning how penguins excel at swimming and diving. I use strong verbs to enhance understanding. I make use of descriptive detail and ask questions that anticipate what you may be thinking (sometimes right at the start of the book).

Many of my books are photo-essays, which use extraordinary photographs to amplify and expand the text, creating different and engaging ways of exploring nonfiction. You'll also find a glossary, an index, and website and research recommendations in most of my books, which make them ideal for enhancing your reading and learning experience. As William Blake wrote in his poem, I want my readers "to see a world in a grain of sand, / And a heaven in a wild flower, / Hold infinity in the palm of your hand, / And eternity in an hour."

Seymour Simon

African elephant at waterhole in Chobe National Park, Botswana

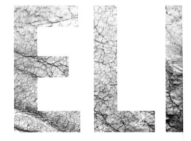

ELI TS

S E Y   M O N

HARPER

An Imprint of HarperCollins*Publishers*

Dedicated to all elephant conservationists.

Photo and Art Credits

Page 2: © Soonthorn Wongsaita / Shutterstock; page 4: © Frans Lanting / MINT Images / Science Source; page 6: © Tony Camacho / Science Source; page 7: © Frans Lanting / MINT Images / Science Source; page 8: © David Hosking / Science Source; page 10: © Bettmann / Getty Images; page 11: © Daniel Eskridge / Stocktrek Images; page 12: © Franki Simonds / Shutterstock; page 13: © J. Wootthisak / Shutterstock; page 14: © Villiers Steyn / Shutterstock; page 17: © David Hosking / Science Source; page 18: © Tony Camacho / Science Source; page 21: © Johan Swanepoel / Shutterstock; page 22: © jono0001/ iStock Photo; page 25: © 1001slide / iStock Photo; page 26, © Mogens Trolle / Shutterstock; page 29: © Pentium2 / iStock Photo; page 30: © Franky Pictures / iStock Photos; page 33: © AP Photo/Bill Sikes; page 34: © PeoGeo / Shutterstock; page 35: © Saravutpics / Shutterstock; page 36: © MHGallery / iStock Photo; page 39: © Magdevski / iStock Photo

Library of Congress Control Number: 2017956243
ISBN 978-0-06-247061-4 (trade bdg.) — ISBN 978-0-06-247060-7 (pbk.)

Typography by Brenda E. Angelilli
18 19 20 21 22 SCP 10 9 8 7 6 5 4 3 2 1
❖
First Edition

Elephants are the largest and heaviest living land animals in the world. They are also one of the most intelligent. Elephants are a huge part of our popular culture and often show up in books, television, and art. They are also associated with wisdom and patience and are famed for their size. One of the most famous elephants was an African elephant who was kept in an English zoo and then an American zoo in the nineteenth century. Its name was Jumbo, which is now used to mean "huge."

At one time, there were dozens of different elephant-like species that lived over most of the world. They lived in deserts, in temperate grasslands, in tropical rainforests, and on snow-covered lands. Nowadays there are far fewer kinds of elephants left in the wild, and all of them are endangered and threatened.

Until 2010, only two living species of elephants were scientifically recognized. But genetic testing has shown that there are at least three different living species of elephants: the African bush elephant, the African forest elephant, and the **Asian elephant**. The African bush elephant lives in Central and southern Africa. The African forest elephant lives in the Congo Basin and West Africa. The Asian elephant lives in South and Southeast Asia.

African elephants are the largest land animals on Earth. They can reach a height of thirteen feet and can weigh up to fifteen thousand pounds. That's heavier than the biggest pickup truck. They have large ears that are fan-shaped, but the forest elephant's are much rounder. Most African elephants, both male and female, have **tusks**. The bush elephant's tusks are large and curved, while the forest elephant's are straighter and point downward. African elephants have two fingerlike lips at the end of their **trunks** that they use to manipulate small objects. The bush elephants are less hairy than the forest elephants, and their foreheads are more rounded.

African forest elephant, Central African Republic

African bush elephants in mist, Ngorongoro Conservation Area, Tanzania

Male Asian elephant, Sri Lanka

Asian elephants are much smaller in size than their African cousins. They have smaller ears and tusks, weigh between six thousand and twelve thousand pounds, and stand six to ten feet high at the shoulder. Still, they are the largest living land animals in Asia. Asian elephants have two prominent bumps on their foreheads and ears that are straight at the bottom. Asian elephants also have dome-shaped backs, and their skin is not as wrinkled as African elephants'. Most elephants are active during dawn and evening hours, although this varies by climate. Modern-day elephants are the only living members of a large group of animals called **Proboscidea**, which are large tusked **mammals** with a flexible trunk.

Drawing of mastodon

Ancient elephants used to number over forty different species. The two best-known species are the mammoths and the mastodons, which became extinct at the end of the last Ice Age, about ten thousand years ago. During the Ice Age, woolly mammoths and mastodons roamed the grassy tundra of the polar regions of the Northern Hemisphere. Early humans lived alongside them and sometimes hunted them for food.

The African elephant is a bit larger than either mastodons or mammoths. For comparison, the modern-day African elephant stands about ten to twelve feet high and weighs four to six tons. Mastodons were about eight to ten feet tall and weighed four to five tons. Mammoths were about nine to eleven feet high and weighed four to six tons. Mastodons were forest browsers. They ate leaves and twigs as well as grasses.

Woolly mammoths had gigantic curling tusks and winter coats of thick hair that reached to the ground. Their tusks were very long, most around nine feet but some as many as fifteen feet. The tusks were used for fighting and to dig up plants in the dirt and under the snow. Their ears were smaller and closer to their heads to keep them warm in the cold climate.

Woolly mammoths are well studied because of the discoveries of their frozen bodies in Siberia and Alaska. They are also pictured in prehistoric paintings on cave walls. One recent finding was of a body of a young woolly mammoth found entombed in Siberian ice near the shores of the Arctic Ocean. Much of its body was still intact and showed marks left from human tools that were used to cut it for food.

Drawing of woolly mammoth

An elephant is covered by a thick **hide** that is leathery and wrinkled. Like most mammals, an elephant also has hair. Its hair is short and stiff and more easily felt than seen. Even though the hide is an inch thick and you would think that it is good insulation, the elephant is still sensitive to high temperatures when out in the sun. Heat is produced inside the huge mass of an elephant's body and given off only at the smaller surface of the skin. Another reason elephants get hot in the sun is that they have very few sweat glands, which would help them to cool down. This is because if they did sweat more, they would need to drink too much water to replace all the water that they lost. The few sweat glands they have are located on their feet between their toes.

In hot weather, the elephant does not stand in the sunlight for extended periods of time. If possible, the elephant moves into the shade of trees or goes into a nearby river or any nearby body of water, including the ocean. Water is important to an elephant. An adult elephant needs to drink many gallons of water every day. Bathing in water also helps keep a bearable body temperature even in hot summers.

If the water it is standing in is not deep enough to cover its whole body, an elephant uses its trunk to spray water over itself. Elephants become very playful in water, splashing themselves and others in the herd. They stamp around in the water, churning up mud, and have a lot of fun. When they are away from water, elephants will spray dust or dirt over their bodies to help protect against the sun.

Elephants bathing, Thailand

An elephant has large feet and thick legs that look like tree trunks. You might think that elephants shake the ground and make a sound like rolling thunder when they walk, but a walking elephant barely makes a sound. An elephant's foot has a tough and fatty pad of connective tissue underneath.

This acts like a spongy shock absorber and spreads out each time an elephant puts its foot down.

Most elephants have five toes but usually four toenails on each round foot. Elephants walk on the tips of their toes, somewhat like ballet dancers in pointed shoes. In fact, a huge elephant makes less of a footprint in soft ground, even with its great weight, than a much lighter person does walking in pointy-heeled shoes. That's because an elephant's foot spreads out the pressure, while pointy heels concentrate the pressure of a person's weight.

If you measure the circumference of an elephant's footprint and multiply it by two, you would be able to tell the elephant's approximate height. For example, if the circumference of an elephant's footprint is forty-eight inches, the elephant would be approximately ninety-six inches high, about eight feet in height.

The sole of an elephant's foot is padded and thick. Because an elephant is constantly walking as it eats, the sole and the toenails wear down. Instead of wearing down smoothly, the soles of elephants' feet remain ridged and cracked. They grip the ground like the ridges on the soles of hiking boots. This helps elephants stay surefooted on hills and bumpy terrain.

Elephants are so easily recognized by most people because of their unmistakable trunks. Scientists call it the "proboscis" (meaning "nose"), but the long, flexible trunk is really the elephant's nose *and* upper lip.

Imagine how you would feel if your nose ran down your face like an arm and you could use it to sniff out food, grab it, and then, if you like the smell, pop it into your mouth. Imagine if you could lift a friend up with your nose, or use your nose to splash water over your body or all over your family. An elephant can do all that and more with its trunk.

An elephant's trunk is muscular, thick, and well protected on the outside and sensitive and delicate on the inside. It has no bones at all and is only made of muscle. It is flexible, can move up and down and side to side, and can even extend in length. The tip of the trunk has one or two lobes that are used like fingers to pick up small objects. The Asian elephants have one on the top, while the African elephants have one on the top and one on the bottom. When an elephant feeds, it uses its trunk like an arm and hand, bringing food to its mouth.

The elephant doesn't drink through its trunk, but it does use its trunk to help it drink. It sucks up water, using the trunk like a straw, and then squirts it into its mouth. The trunk is also used to smell and identify odors from nearby or far away. The trunk can be used like a hand, tenderly, to express affection. And it can be used in anger to fight with other elephants. It can even be used delicately to wipe dust out of another elephant's eye. One of the most fascinating organs in the animal kingdom, an elephant's trunk can do many amazing things.

African forest elephant and calf in the Ngorongoro Conservation Area, Tanzania

An elephant's tusks are its incisor teeth—like the pointy teeth on either side of your mouth. In a way, elephants use their tusks like teeth—to dig in the ground for water and food—but they also use them to lift things and for defense. The incisors present at an elephant's birth grow into "milk" tusks and then fall out after a year when they are about two inches long.

While human teeth are made of dentine, tusks are made of **ivory**. Other animals that have ivory tusks are walruses and sperm whales, but the ivory of an elephant's tusks is much more valuable. Unfortunately, elephants are often hunted and killed by **poachers** just for their tusks, which are prized as art objects. Poaching is the illegal hunting of wild animals.

In humans and in most other animals, teeth come in at both the top and bottom of the mouth. Humans are born toothless, grow a set of baby teeth, called "milk teeth," and finally lose them as they grow adult teeth. Elephants are born without tusks, grow baby (milk) tusks, and replace them with adult tusks. Like you, elephants use molar teeth to grind down their food. In elephants, molar teeth develop in the back of their mouths and push forward as they are used. An elephant has six sets of molars that develop during its lifetime. As each set wears down through constant grinding of food each day, another set pushes forward to take its place toward the front of the mouth.

Losing the last set of molars makes it difficult for an older elephant to chew down and digest enough food and often signals the beginning of the end of its life. Older elephants prefer the softer plant foods found in marshes and swamps, so they often go there to live out their last years.

In the wild, elephants eat almost any kind of plants—including grass, leaves, twigs, shrubs, fruits, bamboo stalks, and bananas. Their main food is grass, along with leaves from trees and bushes. This diet is not a problem in the rainy season when grass and leaves are plentiful, but during a drought it becomes harder to find food. That's when elephants have to find and eat any plant food they can—knocking down trees to eat high foliage and using their tusks to uproot bushes and small trees. They use their tusks to dig in the earth for water as well.

Elephants eat a massive amount. An African elephant eats as much as 660 pounds in a day. The smaller Asian elephant eats less, about 330 pounds a day. Contrast that to a human adult who eats about four pounds of food a day. In nature, elephants spend most of their lives either looking for food or eating it.

Elephants also need to drink huge amounts of water. An African elephant drinks as much as fifty to sixty gallons of water in a single day. That's about as much as a bathtub full of water. Because elephants need to drink so often and so much, they can never live far away from water. That's why even though they may live in different places, from thick jungles to open grasslands, they always have to be near a river, a lake, or just a water hole.

Female elephants (**cows**) and their young (**calves**) live in herds of about ten or so individuals. The leader of the herd is called the **matriarch** and is usually the oldest and most experienced in the group. The matriarch leads the group to find food and water, knows how to avoid lions and other natural **predators**, and remembers locations for shelter. Within the herd, elephants are close-knit and cooperate with each other in many ways.

The females in the herd help each other care for their calves, look for food, and fight common enemies, such as lions. This group may include sisters of the matriarch and their calves. If the herd gets too large, smaller groups may splinter off and form their own groups.

But groups often stay in touch with each other even when they drift miles away from one another. They do this by stamping their feet or making low-frequency sounds. The sounds are so low that people would not be able to hear them.

Male elephants (**bulls**) leave the herd when they become adolescents at about age twelve. Either they will live on their own or form temporary bachelor herds until they become more mature at the age of fifteen or sixteen. Adult bulls sometimes live alone but will visit a herd of females for a short time to breed. Bulls do not care for their calves at all and may live by themselves for much of their lives.

After mating with a male, a female elephant will carry her unborn calf for twenty-two months, a pregnancy (or gestation) that is longer than any other land animal. When born, an elephant calf may be three feet tall and weigh over two hundred pounds. A newborn calf is usually very hairy and has a short trunk and a long tail. It uses its mouth to nurse from its mother, so it doesn't need a long trunk to feed.

Babies are usually blind at birth. They stick close to their mothers and nurse frequently. On average, a calf gains two to three pounds a day during its first year. The other females help the mother to care for the baby, and the entire herd looks after the calf if it is ever in danger.

Even though baby calves are fed and protected, they still have a lot to learn. They stumble around at first, practicing making all four legs work together. By the age of two or three, they are learning how to behave when an enemy, such as a lion, threatens the group. They are taught good elephant manners: Their trunk is held out to an adult elephant in greeting and is also used in "making nice." Calves are taught to use their trunks to wrestle with other calves, to drink water, and for playing "super soakers." Elephant calves may continue nursing for several years until another brother or sister is born. An elephant calf is dependent on its mother and its herd to feed and protect it for three to five years.

Elephants usually eat three times during the day: the late morning, the late afternoon, and the middle of the night. More than half of an elephant's day is taken up by strolling along eating. African bush elephants **graze** mostly on rolling grasslands, whereas smaller African forest elephants **browse** on the leaves and fruits of trees. Asian elephants are both grazers and browsers. They graze on grass during the rainy season and browse on different plants, twigs, and tree bark in forests when the grasses die off. Their food supply depends upon the season.

Elephants don't sleep or rest for more than a few hours at a time. They sleep or rest in the early hours of the morning and in the shade of trees during the heat of the day. Elephants don't have to lie down on the ground when they rest. The straight, strong bones in their legs easily support them while they snooze.

Younger elephant calves amble along with the herd and spend much of their time playing together. Humans play the same games: pushing and tripping each other, climbing over one another, running around wildly after each other. Elephant calves are in danger from natural enemies, such as lions and other big cats and packs of hyenas or wild dogs. When an adult spots danger, it trumpets an alarm. The herd forms a protective ring with the calves inside. Unfortunately, this method doesn't always work against poachers.

Elephants and people have been relating for thousands of years. In the past, elephants were used as carriers of troops and attack animals in war. More than two thousand years ago, the famous Carthaginian general, Hannibal, marched thirty-eight war elephants across the Italian Alps to attack the powerful Roman empire. Hannibal's army nearly won the battle, but only one elephant survived. In Asian countries, such as India, Myanmar, and Thailand, elephants are trained to work. They are not used as pack animals to carry supplies because their backs can't carry more than their weight would suggest. Instead they are used to rip up trees and push objects around.

In some logging and construction camps in Myanmar and Thailand, elephants are taught by their human trainers to use their trunks to lift and push logs and other heavy objects. The bulls learn how to slide their tusks under a log and lift it. Elephants are used in steep and difficult surroundings where trucks and other machinery would slip and slide. But unlike horses and other working animals, elephants are rarely bred for work. Each working elephant is captured in nature, subdued, and trained. Some of these working elephants are well cared for by their keepers—getting days off and plenty of food. But that is not always the case.

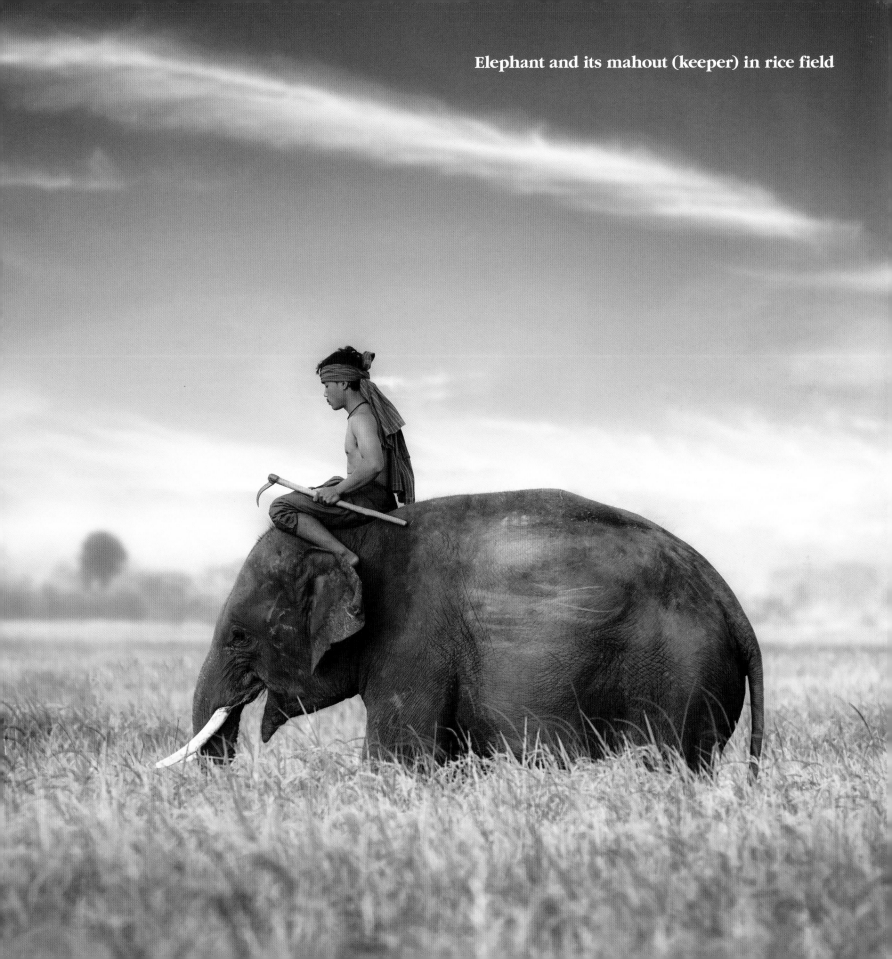

Elephant and its mahout (keeper) in rice field

When elephants are tamed to live or work with humans, it is called **domesticating** them. Elephants in circuses are tamed to be able to parade and carry people, as well as stand on their hind legs and perform in front of audiences. Each domesticated elephant will have its own temperament and personality, and many elephants will not tolerate being treated badly. They will even plan an attack on a cruel or neglectful human keeper. There are many stories of bad keepers being attacked because they weren't giving the elephants proper food and care.

Zoos also keep elephants in many countries around the world. Some of the best zoos put a lot of effort into providing good food and considerable care. This includes paying attention to the social needs of elephants, too—making sure to bond with other elephants and live in a herd. But caring for elephants in captivity is difficult. In the natural world, elephants spend their days roaming over areas of hundreds of square miles, eating as they move, and interacting with other herds and individuals. In zoos, they are confined to smaller spaces and encounter fewer playmates.

Conservation biologists, rangers, and game wardens are recognized for their dedication in service to wildlife, but it is also modern zoological

Elephant herd with Mount Kilimanjaro in the background, Serengeti National Park

institutions, such as the Bronx Zoo, that not only foot the bill in many circumstances but also work diligently behind the scenes to preserve wild animals. A huge elephant and animal reserve in Africa, the Serengeti National Park, would not be there today were it not for Bernhard Grzimek, the former director of Germany's Frankfurt Zoo. Large tracts of African wilderness are also being set aside for wild animals because of the dedicated work of the Wildlife Conservation Society.

Circuses have less space than most zoos. In even the biggest circuses, elephants are confined to small areas. And because of their weight, as well as the acts they are trained to perform in, such as balancing on their hind legs, elephants are at risk for developing painful foot and joint problems.

In recent years, several countries have banned the use of elephants in circuses. A few countries, such as India, have also banned keeping elephants in zoos. In Finland, all the zoos have voluntarily given up keeping elephants because they know that the zoos can't meet elephants' needs. Many people agree and feel it is wrong to keep elephants in captivity for any reason. Many of the larger circuses in the United States no longer use elephants or have shut down because they are no longer using elephants in their acts.

The photo shows an Asian elephant painting on a canvas before the Ringling Bros. and Barnum & Bailey Circus show on Sunday, May 1, 2016, in Providence, Rhode Island, where the elephants performed for the final time. The elephants and other wild animals in the closed-down circus will live at the Ringling Brothers' two-hundred-acre Center for Elephant Conservation in Florida.

Ganesh elephant statue

Humans have always portrayed elephants as big, strong, and intelligent. Many societies show pictures of elephants in their art. Elephants, too, appear in countless stories and legends—from the earliest cave paintings in France, India, and Indonesia dating back forty thousand years to modern photos, paintings, and designs from around the world. Sculptures of elephants are very popular, too.

Both African and Asian elephants are common symbols in religion and folklore. The texts and teachings of religions, including Islam, Buddhism, and Hinduism, contain stories referring to elephants. The Koran tells how a war elephant called Mahmud refused to enter Mecca and prevented it from being conquered. That was the year the prophet Muhammad was born, and it became known as the Year of the Elephant.

In Buddhism, an elephant is a symbol of mental strength and responsibility. Among Hindus, Ganesh is an elephant-headed god that is known as the "remover of obstacles" and is revered for its wisdom. In each religion, the faithful believe that elephants and people share a special bond and are to be treated with respect and care.

Elephant and monk in Surin, Thailand

Elephants are among the most intelligent animals on our planet. Their brains contain even more neurons than a human brain. An adult elephant brain weighs more than ten pounds, much more than any other land animal. Their brains also have many complex folds that are thought to be an important contributor to their high intelligence.

Elephants demonstrate self-awareness and often show emotions, such as grief, compassion, and helplessness. They have excellent learning abilities and quickly understand how to use tools. There are many reports of elephants helping animals of other species, such as rescuing trapped dogs even at considerable cost to their own safety. Younger elephants help older elephants in need. Elephants would be the most dominant land animal on Earth if it were not for people.

Humans are the only real enemies of elephants in the wild. Even in protected nature reserves, poachers and other hunters kill elephants to sell the ivory from their tusks. Preserving elephants and other wild animals isn't an easy task by any means. Land is running short because people continue to build farms and housing on the wild places where elephants live. While some groups are buying land for wild animals, it is a challenge to balance the needs of people and wild animals.

At the beginning of the twenty-first century, there were more than a million African elephants and about forty thousand Asian elephants. In fewer than two decades, there is less than half that population left in the world. Today there are estimates of about a half million African elephants and about thirty-five thousand wild Asian elephants. Animal rights groups estimate that poachers in Africa kill between thirty-five thousand and forty thousand elephants every year. That means about one hundred elephants are killed by poachers every day.

Thanks to the efforts of conservation groups around the world, pressure is put on governments of those countries that have wild elephants to protect them in nature preserves. Will elephants in the wild be saved in the future? It will happen only if enough people want to make it happen.

GLOSSARY

African elephants—Earth's largest land animals. Two kinds exist: the larger African bush elephant and the smaller African forest elephant.

Ancient elephants—Many different kinds of elephant ancestors that existed in the past, including the woolly mammoth and the mastodon.

Asian elephant—The only living kind of elephants that inhabit Asian countries, such as Sri Lanka, India, and Borneo.

Browse—Feeding on high-growing leaves, twigs, and shoots of trees and bushes.

Bull—A male elephant.

Calf—A baby elephant.

Cow—A female elephant.

Domesticated—Animals that have been tamed by humans.

Graze—To feed on grasses and other growing plants.

Hide—An elephant's skin.

Ivory—A hard, white material that comes from the tusks of animals, such as elephants.

Mammal—Animals with backbones that have hair and are warm-blooded. Elephants are mammals.

Matriarch—The female leader of an elephant family. Usually the matriarch is the oldest female.

Poacher—An illegal hunter of elephants.

Predator—Animals that kill other animals for food. Elephant calves are vulnerable to lion and crocodile attacks.

Proboscidea—An order of mammals that includes living elephants and extinct mammoths and mastodons. All have a proboscis, or trunk, they use to handle food and drink water.

Trunk—A fusion of the nose and elephant's upper lip. The trunk can do many things, such as picking up objects and spraying water.

Tusks—The large front teeth that extend well beyond the mouth of an elephant.

INDEX

READ MORE ABOUT IT

Seymour Simon's website
www.seymoursimon.com

National Geographic Kids
www.kids.nationalgeographic.com/animals/african-elephant

World Wildlife Fund
www.worldwildlife.org/species/african-elephant

Defenders of Wildlife
www.defenders.org/elephant/basic-facts